# Steam Heat!
## A Kid's Guide, Port Reykjavik, Iceland

## Photography By John D. Weigand
## Poetry By Penelope Dyan

Bellissima Publishing, LLC
Jamul, California
www.bellissimapublishing.com

Copyright © 2019 by Penny D. Weigand & John D. Weigand

All rights reserved. No part of this book may be reproduced or transmitted in any form or by any means, electronic or mechanical, including photocopying, recording, or by any other means, or by any information or storage retrieval system, without permission from the publisher.

ISBN 978-1-61477-394-8
First Edition

"We come from the earth."

PENELOPE DYAN

# Steam Heat!
## Bellissima Publishing, LLC

# Introduction

As you gaze out at the sites of this most interesting place, you learn the statistics of Iceland from your friendly guide. It seems, you are told, there are only 342,000 inhabitants of this island called Iceland that has run the course all the way from iceberg to tropical, to what we see today; and the amazing thing is they use their natural resources and work in harmony with nature, as they actually run their country on hydro-power and steam heat! This means that electricity is relatively cheap. Even the streets are rid of snow due to pipes of hot water running beneath them! The fact the island sits atop 31 volcanoes makes the tour even more fascinating

Written by the award winning author, attorney and former teacher, Penelope Dyan, this fun, 'learn to read' book filled with word repetition, word recognition and rhyme, is artfully complemented by the photography of John D. Weigand that is certain to amaze and delight! You can travel vicariously with our author and photographer as they explore the layout from the Port of Reykjavik, Iceland. Then when you are all finished reading and exploring vicariously, you can go to the Bellissimavideo YouTube Channel and watch the free music video that goes with this book for even more learning fun!

# Steam Heat!
## Bellissima Publishing, LLC

# Steam Heat!
## A Kid's Guide, Port Reykjavik, Iceland

### Photography By John D. Weigand
### Poetry By Penelope Dyan

You near the Port.
And WHAT comes into view?
It appears that the port is bathed
in green AND blue!

You see a house of yellow.
It's a VERY sun-shiny day,
You wonder of the kids
who live inside THAT house
will come outside and PLAY!

You travel and then you see
a beach of black!
AND in contrast to the water
that is oh so BLUE,
the entire site
seems strange to YOU!

Next you come to a most
unusually interesting PLACE!
You see steam AND bubbling water
all over the place!
Mom explains that (believe it or not)
it is quite TRUE . . .
that if YOU lived HERE in Iceland
THIS is how heat AND electricity
would come to YOU!
"You see," Dad explains,
"from the earth they gather
geothermal power.
And this power lasts FOREVER,
from HOUR to HOUR!"

You watch, as near pool of water
you spy A LOT of steam.
You ask your guide,
"Can making electricity AND heat
be as EASY as it SEEMS?"
Then you are told that the water,
(right along with ALL its heat)
is pumped into pipes
and it goes right down
and right under the STREET!"
Your dad adds,
"Some of the steamy water
is sent to a plant, and it's converted;
and then, you see,
what you end up WITH is electricity!"

And next you learned
that after that (and fairly soon)
the water left over
(from making the electricity)
created a man-made
bright BLUE lagoon!
You see, no matter how hard
the Icelandic people tried and tried,
they could not
(as to Mother Earth)
put that steamy water back inside!

Mom decides to rest on a bench
(that she happens to find)
that has a wall of lava rock
piled high AND right behind . . .
It seems that whether you look HERE
(or whether you look THERE)
you see that volcanic rock
(known as lava)
all over, everywhere!
But that makes sense,
because out of this volcanic earth,
the island of Iceland
was given its BIRTH!

Then, as you move on
(sitting in your bus) of course,
you see the most infamous
Icelandic horse!

You learn there are THREE times
MORE sheep than people
in this land,
And you think that THIS
is VERY, VERY grand!

As the day ends you pass
a sleepy house high upon a hill.
And all of the world seems
very silent and still!

Then Mom decides
that you ALL must stop,
AND she buys you a lamb blanket
AND a toy polar bear
from a nearby souvenir shop!

And finally, as you lay that night
in your 'far away from home' bed,
memories of Mom looking out
at all that water and at all that steam,
fill up YOUR little head.
Under your lamb blanket,
you hold your toy polar bear
VERY, VERY, VERY tight.
Mom kisses your forehead and says,
"Sweet Dreams!" and "Good night!"
You tell Mom,
"I think it is really, really neat,
that Iceland makes electricity
and keeps warm
from the earth's very OWN heat!"

"If you choose to be one with Mother Earth, you will never be cold!"

PENELOPE DYAN